I0159733

"Wisdom That Transforms. Action That Lasts."

The Get Wisdom Commitment

At Get Wisdom Publishing we believe that true wisdom has the power to transform lives. Our mission is to equip readers with timeless insights and practical tools that inspire growth, guide decisions, and empower purposeful living. We don't just inform—we empower.

Our books combine profound understanding with real-life application, enabling readers to unlock their potential and navigate life's challenges with clarity and confidence. With each step guided by wisdom, we help you create lasting change and live the life you deserve.

When wisdom meets purpose, transformation follows.

The *OBSCURE* Bible Study Series

Grow in your faith through investigating unusual and obscure biblical characters.

"Deep Biblical Wisdom. Real-Life Faith Application."

The OBSCURE Bible Study Journey

Meet Shamgar, Jethro, Manoah & Hathach

**An introduction to the unique characters of
The *OBSCURE* Bible Study Series**

**Leader Guide
Book 1**

Discover the overlooked.

Stephen H Berkey

GETWISDOM
PUBLISHING

Available as an audiobook on our Amazon
Obscure Bible Study Series page:

COPYRIGHT

ISBN 978-1-7344094-0-6   (Leader Guide, paperback)

ISBN 978-1-7344094-2-0   (Leader Guide, ebook)

ISBN 978-1-7344094-1-3   (Personal Study Guide, paperback)

ISBN 978-1-7344094-3-7   (Personal Study Guide, ebook)

Audiobook available   (amazon.com and audible.com)

Available as an audiobook on our Amazon
Obscure Bible Study Series page:

Bible Translations Used:

Discover the biblical characters that mainstream studies forget – and the timeless lessons they teach."

TABLE OF CONTENTS

CONTENTS

FREE PDF RESOURCES

Living Wisely
The Life Planning Guide

A Quick-Start Guide to Purposeful Living and Wise Decisions!

Discover the five life domains: purpose, people, principles, productivity, and perspective. Wisdom is the ability to apply truth and logic to real-life decisions and produce good outcomes. It influences your choices and will produce action that lasts. Consider and apply the five practical wisdom principles for daily living. (6 pages)

Free PDF: https://getwisdompublishing.com/resource-registration/

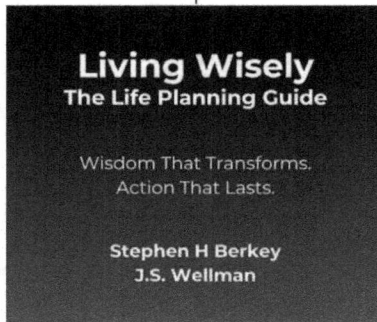

Living Wisely
The Life Planning Guide

Wisdom That Transforms.
Action That Lasts.

Stephen H Berkey
J.S. Wellman

Free PDF

Five Practical Principles For Life

When wisdom meets purpose, transformation follows.

Free PDF
Wise
Decision-Making

[Get the ebook version for 99 cents]

You can make good choices.

This free resource provides a project-oriented perspective and gives ten detailed steps to analyze issues/problems to determine a solution. (26 pages)

Good decisions expand your horizons. Don't allow the fear of decision-making paralyze your ability to make good choices. Think through the alternatives and move forward. When your eyes are on the goal, making good decisions is easier.

Free PDF: https://getwisdompublishing.com/resource-registration/

Kindle ebook for 99 cents: https://www.amazon.com/dp/B09SYGWRVL/

Ebook

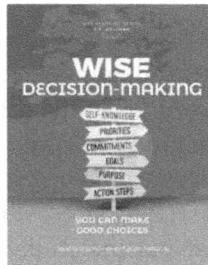

Free PDF

Make Thoughtful Decisions!

Good decisions expand your horizons.

Why Study OBSCURE Characters?

Unique, New, and Fresh

For experienced Bible students these characters will provide a fresh and interesting approach to Bible study. Since most of the material will be unfamiliar to the participants, new believers or those just starting Bible study should not feel intimidated by students who have been studying for years. Most readers will not be acquainted with the majority of the characters and events in this series.

Knowledge of Scripture

These studies are a great introduction for those just beginning Bible study. Regardless of their level of knowledge, everyone should find the characters and stories provide an opportunity to grow in their faith through investigating fascinating and unusual biblical stories and incidents.

Valuable Life Lessons

These lesser-known characters are a lot like you and me. God uses all sorts of people to accomplish His plans! You will become familiar with ordinary people, strange characters, and people living on the fringe of life who have the same troubles and challenges as people today. The deep truths and life lessons embedded in these studies should be valuable.

Intended Audience

GROUPS: This study series should make it easy to recruit people to small group meetings. Everyone in the group will be at the same place, having little information or background about the story.
PERSONAL: Individual believers looking for something different should find this series of studies interesting and challenging because the questions will put the student into the story and ask, "What are you feeling, or doing?" Or, "What do you need to do?"
CHURCH: Selected lessons or books would make for an interesting sermon series or a church-wide study.

"Unlock Biblical Wisdom.
Transform Your faith!"

ABOUT THE LEADER GUIDE

General

This Guide is designed to give the Leader adequate information to effectively lead a discussion of each lesson. It contains additional information and background and follow-up questions.

You do <u>not</u> need to be a Bible student or mature Christian, to lead a group discussion with this Guide.

All you need is a desire and basic group facilitating skills. You simply need to read the questions aloud and keep the group discussion on target.

We recommend that you begin the discussion by reading the provided Scripture. This will allow time for everyone to get settled. It will remind everyone of the subject and bring their minds to a common focus. We do not believe ice-breakers are necessary given the unique nature of the material. If you sense that the group needs additional focus before you begin, conduct a <u>short</u> discussion about the themes of the lesson or ask about the meaning of a particular term.

Goals

The discussion should center around the themes and application questions at the end of the lesson. Your goal as the Leader should be to foster understanding and familiarity with Scripture. For new believers or participants who are not comfortable with the Bible, your goal should be to help them begin to seek knowledge and understanding from His Word. Try to get participants to put themselves into the lives of the *OBSCURE* character and feel what that character is feeling, thinking, or believing. More mature participants have the opportunity to dig deeper and find personal meaning and understanding. They may be particularly impacted by the Application questions.

Prayer

Unless you have an outstanding person of prayer in your group, you as the leader should wrap up your discussion time with prayer that specifically reflects the discussion and the themes, purpose, and focus of the lesson.

"Discover the Overlooked.
Apply it to Your Life!"

Book Description

Discover Your Divine Purpose:
Lessons from Forgotten Biblical Heroes

Are you searching for clarity and purpose in your life? Do you feel like you're just going through the motions, longing for a deeper connection to God's plan?

The OBSCURE Bible Study Series invites you to explore the lives of often-overlooked figures of the Bible, revealing the timeless wisdom hidden within their stories. These books equip you with actionable tools to transform your life through focused biblical wisdom and everyday faith application.

Learn how God works through ordinary people to accomplish extraordinary things and discover the clarity and direction you need to align your life with His purpose. Gain insights into your unique spiritual gifts, experience spiritual renewal, and find the freedom that comes from surrendering your plans to God's perfect will. This isn't just a devotional; it's a journey into biblical wisdom in action.

As you delve into the stories of this introductory volume you will meet Shamgar, Jethro, Manoah and Hathach, and find biblical insights others have missed. Small group meetings will bring fresh perspectives to your studies. You can bridge the gap between biblical knowledge and everyday wisdom.

God frequently uses the unknown and the obscure to make a point. Most of the Bible's major characters were simple, everyday, common people. Although there are some exceptions, most were not rich or famous. Sometimes those who put in only a brief appearance contribute in very special and significant ways to building the Kingdom.

Most of the people chosen for these studies are unfamiliar because they were mentioned only a few times in Scripture – some only once. Others may have more recognizable names but their contribution is obscure. A few more should be familiar (even very familiar) and are included because of their unique or particular contribution to kingdom work.

For example, Shamgar is mentioned only twice in the Bible. Judges 3:31 tells his story and 5:6 simply establishes a timeline and says nothing more about him. Shamgar was a contemporary of Deborah. Judges 3:31 says that he killed 600 Philistines with his oxgoad. If I were Shamgar and I killed 600 Philistines with a stick, I would be hoping for a little more coverage than one verse!

Then there is Nicodemus, with whom we associate the concept of being "born again." His name appears only 5 times in the Scriptures, all in one short passage in the book of John.

Eve, although not really obscure, is included in the Series in order to investigate the creation story.

One might think that studying these people is not really worthwhile. But that's a faulty conclusion. In total they tell the story of the Bible and the Gospel in a very interesting, fresh, and challenging way. Each study has one or more major themes.

The complete study series provides a relatively complete overview of most of the major topics in the Christian faith.

"Scripture holds answers in unexpected places. Our unique Bible studies reveal overlooked wisdom for today's challenges."

INTRODUCTION

We equip readers with timeless wisdom and practical tools
that transform, not just inform. Our books combine
deep insights with real-life application
to create lasting change.

Description of The OBSCURE Bible Study Series

This unique series uses a number of lesser-known Bible characters and events to explore such major themes as Angels, being Born Again, Courage, Death, Evangelism, Faithfulness, Forgiveness, Grace, Hell, Leadership, Miracles, the Remnant, the Sabbath, Salvation, Rebellion, Sovereignty, Thankfulness, Women, the World, Creation, and End Times.

The series as a whole provides both a broad and fresh understanding of the nature of God as we see Him act in the lives of people we've never examined before.

Group Discussion or Individual Study

These studies can be done individually or in a small discussion group. The real value of the study is in the discussion questions. We all see life differently and the thoughts and ideas shared in a group will often lead to a richer understanding of the Scripture. The questions often require the participant to put himself (herself) in the mind or circumstances of that person in the Scriptures.

The commentary portion of the introductory material in each lesson is there to help clarify the passage and set the stage for the discussion questions. The questions are designed to help the student understand the meaning of the text itself and explore the kingdom implications from a personal point of view.

Ideal For Both New and Mature Bible Students

These lessons have three underlying questions:

- "Who is this person?"
- "What is happening here?"
- "What is the implication for my life?"

Because of the obscurity of the characters under study, chances are that even experienced participants with prior understanding of the lesson's theme will find fresh material to explore. Both new and long-time students will be challenged by the life lessons these unfamiliar characters can teach them.

Format of Lessons

Each lesson begins with the Scripture using the ESV translation followed by short sections titled "Context," "What Do We Know," and "Observations." The discussion questions are designed to help the student understand the subject and are followed by several application questions.

Number of Lessons
There are 9 books in the *OBSCURE* series with 68 individual lessons.

"We believe applied wisdom empowers life change. Our books provide clarity, inspiration, and tools to equip readers to live their best life."

Shamgar
the lone warrior judge

Occurrences of "Shamgar" in the Bible: 2

Themes: Courage; Involvement

Scripture

Judges 3:31   *After him [Ehud] was Shamgar the son of Anath, who killed 600 of the Philistines with an oxgoad, and he also saved Israel.* ESV

Judges 3:31   *After Ehud, Shamgar son of Anath, became judge, He delivered Israel by striking down 600 Philistines with an oxgoad.* HCSB

Judges 5:6-7   *In the days of Shamgar, son of Anath, in the days of Jael, the highways were abandoned, and travelers kept to the byways. 7 The villagers ceased in Israel; they ceased to be until I arose; I, Deborah, arose as a mother in Israel.* ESV

> NOTE: This is part of Deborah's Song of celebration (Judges 5) that she and Barak sang in response to their victory over the Canaanites.

The Context

Judges were men or women raised up by God to deliver Israel from her enemies. They were often charismatic leaders who would rally Israel to defeat or drive out invaders. They were God's agents to free Israel during times of oppression from neighboring kings, city-states or nations.

Shamgar is one of the "minor" judges because very little is said about his tenure as a judge. Shamgar has one little verse in the Bible – that's it! He kills 600 men with a stick and he only gets one verse. Our challenge is to see what we can learn from one verse.

Shamgar became a judge after Ehud and before Deborah, or during the time of Deborah. Shamgar's story is almost humorous because his one verse appears at the end of the chapter describing another judge, Ehud. The chapter ends with this verse and then Chapter 4 begins describing the time of Deborah. Nothing more is said of Shamgar and his life. I find this both strange and interesting at the same time.

During the time of Ehud, "the people of Israel again did what was evil in the sight of the Lord . . ." (Judges 3:12). Ehud rescued Israel and the land was at peace for 80 years until he died. Then Shamgar became a judge, killed 600 Philistines, and delivered Israel again. The first verse of Chapter 4 leading into the story about Deborah and Barak tells us that the Israelites again did what was evil in the sight of the Lord. The Scripture then tells about the exploits of Deborah. Shamgar's service to Israel is not mentioned again in any way, except for the reference in 5:6-7.

What Do We Not Know?

How, when, where, and why Shamgar killed 600 Philistines is basically unknown. Yes, he used his oxgoad, but that doesn't tell us much, other than he turned a farm implement into a weapon. It is not clear why this verse is inserted here because no details are provided to give us any hint as to what happened.

Therefore, let's begin by listing what we do _not_ know:

> ***NOTE to LEADER:** The purpose of this list is to provide context to the participants. If you start your discussion talking about this list of what we don't know, it will likely disrupt or derail the flow of the discussion questions. If participants start raising these questions, encourage them to wait until the end.

1. We don't know over what period of time these 600 men were killed. If they had all been killed in one big battle one would assume that more details of Shamgar's strength, courage, or cunning would be provided.

2. If God had assisted Shamgar in some way, one would assume that the author would want to preserve that fact in order to give God the credit, but nothing is said about how the 600 were killed.

3. It's possible the circumstances of how these men were killed is an embarrassment to Israel, so the writer simply mentions the situation and provides no details. Maybe they were killed against the wishes or instructions of God, or maybe they were killed in a manner not pleasing to God.

4. It's not clear how this many men could be killed with an oxgoad. It's possible one could beat someone to death, but it would take some time and the enemy would surely kill or capture the attacker in the process. It's possible the oxgoad had been sharpened and used like a spear, but even that would not explain how 600 men could be killed.

5. Given the nature of the weapon and the number of men killed, one might conclude that the Philistines were drugged or speared to death in their sleep. But even that sounds incredible.

6. The most likely scenario is that these men were killed over a long period of time in many battles or individual encounters.

7. We don't know whether the 600 were killed when only Shamgar was present or whether Shamgar was involved in a number of battles with other soldiers helping him and he received the credit because he was the leader.

8. We don't know if the large number of kills is the result of extraordinary courage and bravery or the result of deception, shrewdness, and lies.

9. We don't know how Shamgar became a judge and if he attacked the Philistines on his own or if he was following God's orders and using God's battle plan.

10. We really don't know how significant the killing of the 600 Philistines is because we don't know any of the circumstances. It might have been in insignificant little battles over a period of months (perhaps many months). The author simply states it at the end of Chapter 3 and then moves on to the story of Deborah.

11. We don't know how long this campaign allowed Israel to live in peace, if at all.

12. The entire situation with the Philistines and the deserted road and villages may have been only a local situation, and so wasn't worth providing any more information.

WE DON'T KNOW MUCH, DO WE?

What Do We Know?

Based on the Holman translation (HCSB), we know eight facts:

1) Shamgar was a "**judge**,"
2) Shamgar "**delivered**" Israel,
3) The "delivery" **did not last** long,
4) Shangar killed **600** Philistines,
5) He used an **oxgoad**,
6) Shamgar was the **son of Anath**,
7) The main **roads were deserted**, and
   (travelers kept to side roads)
8) The **villages were deserted**.

Discussion Questions

A. HISTORICAL CONTEXT

A1. What is the general timeframe of the period of the Judges?

*After the death of Joshua and before the appointment of Saul and then David as King.
*During the period of the judges, from about 1380 B.C. - 1050 B.C., the government of Israel was a loose

confederation of tribes gathered about their central shrine, the ark of the covenant.

A2. What was the major problem of those days that was re-stated throughout Judges like a catch phrase?

*Judges 17:6   *In those days there was no king in Israel. Everyone did what was right in his own eyes.*   ESV

A3. There was a pattern of behavior in those days that kept repeating itself. What was it?

*THE PATTERN: People were faithful – people sinned and rebelled against God – God disciplined the people by sending oppressors – people cried out to God – God raised up a deliverer (judge) – the judge delivered the people from the oppression.

A high moral and religious point at the beginning, but that was followed by a downward spiral of sin and rebellion so that by the end of the book Israel looked just like the pagans they were living among – defiled, unfaithful, and wicked.

The book demonstrates what happens to men when they can do whatever they want → moral and spiritual chaos. It shows what happens when God's people allow the world to dictate their lives rather than God. Israel almost forgot Yahweh.

A4. What did the people demand from God? Why?

*A King! Other nations had a King.
*Judges 8:22-23   *Then the men of Israel said to Gideon, "Rule over us, you and your son and your grandson also, for you have saved us from the hand of Midian." 23 Gideon said to them, "I will not rule over you, and my son will not rule over you; the Lord will rule over you."* ESV

*JUDGES: Without a human king/leader to guide them, the people tended to rebel and fall into worship of false gods time and time again. "Everyone did what was right in his own eyes" (Judges 17:6; 21:25). These were chaotic times. To punish the people, God would send foreign nations or tribes to oppress the Israelites.[1] (Nelson's)

B. WHAT WE KNOW – EIGHT FACTS

B1. Shamgar was a "judge."

B1a. What was a "judge"?

*Judges were men or women raised up by God to deliver Israel from her enemies. They were often charismatic leaders who would rally Israel to defeat or drive out invaders. They were God's agents to free Israel during times of oppression from neighboring kings, city-states or nations.

These judges or leaders would rally the people to defeat the enemy. As God's agents for justice and deliverance, they would act decisively to free the nation from oppression. But the judges themselves were often weak, and results of their works were short-lived. The people would enter another stage of rebellion, only to see the cycle of oppression and deliverance repeated all over again.[2] (Nelson's)

NOTE: There are 15 judges identified in the Bible. Six of them are considered minor judges because little is said about them and they may have been active during times when other judges were also serving. The judge did not necessarily rule over the entire area of Israel but often over a specific smaller geographic area which I suspect was the case for Shamgar. The other minor judges are Tola (10:1-2); Jair (10:3-5); Ibzan (12:8-11); Elon (12:11-13); and Abdon (12:13-15). The well-known judges are Deborah, Gideon, and Samson.

B1b. How do we know Shamgar was a judge? If I said that Shamgar was not really a judge, how would you respond?

>   *It is never stated in many translations (KJV, NASB, ESV, NIV) that Shamgar was a judge.
>   *The Hebrew text for 3:31 does not say he was a judge.
>   *Holman appears alone in its translation.

B1c. Was Shamgar appointed or raised up by God?

>   *Don't know!
>   *There is no evidence that he was appointed by God.
>   *He just appears in the text between Ehud and Deborah.
>   *3:31 does not include any of the normal information about judges, for example: divine calling, tribal affiliation, geographical details, duration of rule, and place of burial.

B1d. What is the best evidence that he was a judge?

>   *He is mentioned in the text after Ehud.
>   *Text says he "delivered" Israel.
>   *Historically thought of as a minor judge.
>   *He performed a heroic feat.
>   *He is mentioned by Deborah (but, he is associated with a non-judge, Jael). This may be stronger evidence that Shamgar was not really a judge.

B2. Shamgar "delivered" Israel.

B2a. The text says that he "delivered" Israel. What do you think that means?

>   *What did he deliver them from? Unsafe deserted roads?
>   *Probably freed from Philistine domination.
>   *Probably just a local operation versus leading all of Israel.

B2b. Is there any evidence that Shamgar acted in any ruling or leadership capacity?

>   *No, there is no evidence that Shamgar did any ruling or leading – just a mighty warrior who killed 600 Philistines.

B2c. The judges were to be rescuers and leaders. What characteristics would you want in a leader if you lived in those days?

>   *Peace and safety.
>   *These were strange days because there were no longer strong leaders in charge after Moses and Joshua.
>   *Result was: the people did whatever they wanted.

B3. The "delivery" did not last long.

B3a. Do you think Shamgar's reign as a judge was successful? Why? Why not?

>   *PRIOR VERSE: (3:30) says that after Ehud's victory over the Moabites, they had peace for 80 years. Then first verse after 3:31 says the Israelites once again did evil in the eyes of the Lord.
>   *Probably not – Judges 5:6-7 . . . *they were deserted in Israel, until I, Deborah, I arose, a mother in Israel.*

B4. Killed 600 Philistines

Many assume this verse implies there was no army, no support troops, no chariots, etc. Do you think Shamgar did this alone or was he part of a group? Why? Why not?

>   *600 is a round number; probably not meant to be specific.
>   *Feat almost requires God (if against Philistine warriors) and there is no mention of God.

B5. With an oxgoad.

B5a. What is an oxgoad?

>   *The goad used by the Syrian farmer is usually a straight
>   branch of oak or other strong wood (usually about 10 feet
>   long) from which the bark has been stripped, and which
>   has at one end a pointed spike and at the other a flat
>   chisel-shaped iron. The pointed end is to prod the oxen
>   while plowing. The flattened iron at the other end is to
>   scrape off the earth which clogs the plowshare.[3] (ISBE)

B5b. How do you kill 600 people with a stick?

>   *Oxgoad converted to weapon.
>   *Possiblty not killed at one time but over a period of time
>   in many battles/confrontations.
>   *Possibly Shamgar had help and because he was the leader
>   he got all the credit.
>   *He may have had God's supernatural help.
>   *Maybe killed the 600 in their sleep.
>   *Some special circumstances: ambush, Philistines
>   incapacitated in some way.

B5c. Why an oxgoad? Why not use a real weapon? Normally the
weapons used in a battle would not be mentioned. Why do you
think the oxgoad is mentioned in this verse?

>   *They had no real weapons – Philistines had confiscated
>   them.
>   *1 Sam 13:19, 22   *Now there was no blacksmith to be found
>   throughout all the land of Israel, for the Philistines said, "Lest the
>   Hebrews make themselves swords or spears." . . . 22 So on the
>   day of the battle there was neither sword nor spear found in the
>   hand of any of the people with Saul and Jonathan, but Saul and
>   Jonathan his son had them.* ESV

B6. Son of Anath

B6a. If you simply read this text, what do you naturally assume that "son of Anath" means?

> *Family.
> *But, *Anath* is not a Hebrew name.

HOME LOCATION: Some believe Anath is a contraction of *Beth Anath*, an ancient fortified city of the Canaanites. If true, then Anath may be the city from which Shamgar came, and not his father. This is similar to Moses saying, "I am a son of Israel."[4 (Nelson's)]

WARRIOR: Anath is also connected with the Phoenician and Canaanite goddess Anat, who was worshipped in Egypt. She is coupled with the war-goddess Astart. The goddess Anath (the sister and consort of Baal) appears in Ugaritic literature as the goddess of war as well as of love. Thus, the phrase "Shamgar ben Anath," could possibly mean "Shamgar, the warrior."[5 (ISBE)]

B6b. If either of the above is true, what is one obvious conclusion?

> *Shamgar is not an Israelite.

B6c. If Shamgar was not an Israelite, and maybe not even a follower of Yahweh, what might this explain?

> *The reason that Shamgar gets very little mention concerning his exploits in Israel.
> *He was not part of the family of God, the Israelites.

B6d. Were there any "rules" about judges that would prevent a foreigner from acting in that capacity?

> *Apparently not. The only rule was the sovereignty of God.
> *God raised up the judges.
> *We really don't know for sure that God appointed Shamgar as a judge!

B6e. Do you think it makes any difference that Shamgar may have been a foreigner and not a Hebrew?

> *No, the judges were not necessarily spiritual leaders. They were warriors who freed Israel from oppression.
> *The priests would have been the spiritual leaders.
> *God could have used Shamgar simply as an instrument to help keep the main road safe etc., and he was not really involved in leadership.

B6f. Does being a foreigner or a pagan have any special implications here?

> *It was the foreigners (or native inhabitants) who were oppressing them.
> *God may have used one of their own against them.

B6g. If Shamgar was a foreigner and a pagan, why would he choose to act as a deliverer for Israel? Why would God choose and use a foreigner?

> *Try to shame Israel. They could not do it themselves, thus, must rely on a foreigner.
> *Gentiles are not necessarily all evil and bad - except the Canaanites.
> *It was a minor skirmish in God's overall plan and Shamgar was available.

B7. Main roads and villages deserted

This is the only hint of information as to why Shamgar killed the Philistines and it is only an assumption because Deborah mentioned the problem in her song. But the problem also existed during the days of Jael.

B7a. Do you think this is a big enough problem to warrant one warrior killing 600 Philistines?

>
> *Hard to say.
> *If truly deserted the problem had to be significant.

B7b. Given what you know about where the Philistines and Israelites settled, other than dangerous conditions, why else might the roads be deserted?

>
> *The Israelites had originally taken the high country.

B8. Interesting speculation:

The limited information about Shamgar has led to a great deal of speculation because it raises a number of problems for Old Testament historians. The entry at 3:31 almost seems like an afterthought. Maybe the author, after seeing Deborah's reference in her song (5:6), went back and inserted 3:31 in order to make the text complete.

B8a. Do you think the lack of information is because Shamgar was a "minor judge?" If not, then how do you explain?

>
> *No – arguing that Shamgar was only a minor judge does not change or explain the lack of information.
> *Maybe there was something embarrassing about the story that the author did not want to repeat.
> *Maybe Shamgar was a Canaanite.
> *Maybe the killings were not sanctioned by God.
> *Maybe it was ineffective in solving the bigger problem with the Philistines and there was overlap with Deborah.
> *Maybe Shamgar was unknown to later editors, but since Deborah mentioned, it is inserted with a heroic feat.
>
> *Some scholars identify the similarities between the heroic feat of Shamgar and other military exploits in the OT (e.g., those of the "mighty men" of David in 2 Sam 21:15-22;

23:8-12, and especially Samson's slaughter of a thousand Philistines at Lehi with the jaw-bone of an ass, Judg 15:14), leading to the conclusion that Shamgar was inserted in the list of judges and supplied with a suitable heroic feat in order to provide some background for an otherwise unknown figure (or at least unknown to the later redactor who inserted 3:31).[6] [(ISBE)]

*SPECULATION: Several writers have challenged the Biblical account on the following grounds: that in Judg 5 no mention is made of any deliverance; that the name "Shamgar" resembles the name of a Hittite king and the name "Anath" that of a Syrian goddess; that the deed recorded in Judg 3:31 is analogous to that of Samson (Judg 15:15), and that of Shammah, son of Agee (2 Sam 23:11 f); and lastly, that in a group of old Greek manuscripts and other versions, this verse is inserted after the account of Samson's exploits. None of these is necessarily inconsistent with the traditional account. Nevertheless, they have been used as a basis not only for overthrowing the tradition, but also for constructive theories such as that which makes Shamgar a foreign oppressor and not a judge, and even the father of Sisera.[7] [(ISBE)]

C. CONCLUSION

C1. Since we have so little information and if we believe nothing happens by accident with God, then there must be some good reason why the story of Shamgar appears here. What do you think that could be? If this story were not included in the Bible, what would be the impact? If your answer is "nothing," then why is the verse here? Why do <u>you</u> think this verse is here? What is <u>your</u> thoughtful view?

C2. What did <u>you</u> find most interesting or curious about this story?

C3. How do you see God at work in this story?

   *If someone kills 600 of the enemy with a stick – he would
    have needed God's help!

D. APPLICATION

Too little is known to make many definitive observations. But the
story does afford the opportunity for some interesting and
challenging sermon topics:

   1. God will use anybody He needs to accomplish His
   purposes.
   2. If you are called on to "fight" for God, use what you
   know and what you have available to you.
   3. The battle can be won despite incredible odds if God is
   on your side.
   4. Do you need to pick up your oxgoad and get in the
   battle?
   5. What oxgoad has God given you? What are your
   spiritual gifts? You could be using them as a weapon!
   6. Is it time to attack the oppressor in our midst?
   7. If God was looking for another Shamgar, how would He
   find you? Are you ready? Are you available?

D1. Which one of the above do you like the best and why? Do any
of the sermon subjects nick at your heart? Is God speaking to you
in any of these topics?

D2. What "oxgoad" has God given you? What does God want you
doing with your tools? Is it time for you to pick up your oxgoad?

D3. If you did decide God is nudging you, what would that look like?

E. CHALLENGE EXERCISE

Chose one of the preaching topics listed above and develop a three point sermon outline. An example for #4: "Do you need to pick up your oxgoad and get in the battle?"

1) What are you presently doing for God?

2) Are you making a difference?

3) What legacy will you leave?

Jethro
Moses' father-in-law

Occurrences of "Jethro" in the Bible: 10
Jethro's name occurs only ten times (eight times in Exodus 18) but he is identified several more times in Exodus 18 as Moses' "father-in-law."

Theme: Leadership

*Special Note to LEADER: This lesson, by its nature, will be a little longer than most. Plan your time accordingly.

Scripture

Exodus 18:5-27
Jethro, Moses' father-in-law, came with his sons and his wife to Moses in the wilderness where he was encamped at the mountain of God. 6 And when he sent word to Moses, "I, your father-in-law Jethro, am coming to you with your wife and her two sons with her," 7 Moses went out to meet his father-in-law and bowed down and kissed him. And they asked each other of their welfare and went into the tent. 8 Then Moses told his father-in-law all that the Lord had done to Pharaoh and to the Egyptians for Israel's sake, all the hardship that had come upon them in the way, and how the Lord had delivered them. 9 And Jethro rejoiced for all the good that the Lord had done to Israel, in that he had delivered them out of the hand of the Egyptians.

10 Jethro said, "Blessed be the Lord, who has delivered you out of the hand of the Egyptians and out of the hand of Pharaoh and has delivered the people from under the hand of the Egyptians. 11 Now I know that the Lord is greater than all gods, because in this affair they dealt arrogantly with the people." 12 And Jethro, Moses' father-in-law, brought a burnt offering and sacrifices to God; and

Aaron came with all the elders of Israel to eat bread with Moses' father-in-law before God.

13 The next day Moses sat to judge the people, and the people stood around Moses from morning till evening. 14 When Moses' father-in-law saw all that he was doing for the people, he said, "What is this that you are doing for the people? Why do you sit alone, and all the people stand around you from morning till evening?" 15 And Moses said to his father-in-law, "Because the people come to me to inquire of God; 16 when they have a dispute, they come to me and I decide between one person and another, and I make them know the statutes of God and his laws." 17 Moses' father-in-law said to him, "What you are doing is not good. 18 You and the people with you will certainly wear yourselves out, for the thing is too heavy for you. You are not able to do it alone. 19 Now obey my voice; I will give you advice, and God be with you! You shall represent the people before God and bring their cases to God, 20 and you shall warn them about the statutes and the laws, and make them know the way in which they must walk and what they must do. 21 Moreover, look for able men from all the people, men who fear God, who are trustworthy and hate a bribe, and place such men over the people as chiefs of thousands, of hundreds, of fifties, and of tens. 22 And let them judge the people at all times. Every great matter they shall bring to you, but any small matter they shall decide themselves. So it will be easier for you, and they will bear the burden with you. 23 If you do this, God will direct you, you will be able to endure, and all this people also will go to their place in peace."

24 So Moses listened to the voice of his father-in-law and did all that he had said. 25 Moses chose able men out of all Israel and made them heads over the people, chiefs of thousands, of hundreds, of fifties, and of tens. 26 And they judged the people at all times. Any hard case they brought to Moses, but any small matter they decided themselves. 27 Then Moses let his father-in-law depart, and he went away to his own country.   ESV

The Context

Moses had become friends with Jethro after traveling to Midian. Moses married one of Jethro's daughters and settled down as a shepherd. Then God called Moses to save Israel and in the process of challenging Pharaoh and leading Israel out of slavery, Moses sent his wife and children back to be with her father. Moses freed Israel from slavery, led them across the Red Sea, and the entire nation of more than 2 million plus made its way toward Mt. Sinai.

Jethro heard about what Moses had been doing as he approached Mount Sinai. Jethro decided to visit and return Moses' family, now that he was safely out of Egypt. Israel had not yet reached Mount Sinai where they would be given the Ten Commandments and all the other provisions of the Law. Chapter 18 tells us what happened when the two men met and about the godly advice Jethro gave Moses.

What Do We Know?

In 18:1 we learn that Jethro was a pagan priest of some kind. But then it is reported that Jethro participated with Moses in worshiping Yahweh. The logical conclusion is that Jethro was converted to faith in Moses' God:

1) 18:9   Jethro rejoiced over what the Lord had done for Israel
2) 18:10   He praised the Lord
3) 18:11   He recognized who God is, referred to Him as Yahweh
4) 18:12a   He brought a burnt offering to Yahweh
5) 18:12b   They ate a meal in God's presence with elders

The rest of this chapter provides an outline of twelve life or leadership principles we should all know and understand. Jethro was the one giving Moses advice in most situations, and Moses was mature enough to listen, consider, and implement the wise direction Jethro provided. This advice is probably best described as fatherly instruction, but it also represents principles that should be followed in all our lives, particularly if we are leaders of any kind. The advice can be used in families, churches, work environments, governments, etc.

Leadership Principles[8]

Principle #1: Mutual Respect

Exodus 18:5-7   *Jethro, Moses' father-in-law, came with his sons and his wife to Moses in the wilderness . . . 6 And when he sent word to Moses, "I, your father-in-law Jethro, am coming to you . . ." 7 Moses went out to meet his father-in-law and bowed down and kissed him. And they asked each other of their welfare and went into the tent. ESV*

1A. What actions did Moses and Jethro take that demonstrated mutual respect?

> *Moses went to meet him, not waiting for him to arrive.
> *Moses humbly bowed and kissed him.
> *Jethro invited him into his tent.

1B. Why did Jethro send Moses notice that he was outside the camp? Why didn't he just come into the camp? What are the possible scenarios if Jethro had come into Moses' camp without advance warning and demanded to see Moses? What would have been a possible greeting by Moses and his leaders?

> NOTICE:
> *He demonstrated he had come in peace.
> *Moses or his people could be mistaken about the reason Jethro is there.
> IF NO NOTICE:
> *Suspicion.
> *Think bringing bad news.
> POSSIBLE RECEPTION:
> *Might have met them with weapons.
> *Prevent them from entering.

1C. Other than respect, what did Moses demonstrate by going out to meet Jethro?

*Honor of Jethro. He made Jethro look good in the eyes of Jethro's people.
*Send message that Jethro deserves respect.

Principle #2: Attitude of Gratitude and Thanksgiving

Exodus 18:9-12   *And Jethro rejoiced for all the good that the Lord had done to Israel, in that he had delivered them out of the hand of the Egyptians. 10 Jethro said, "Blessed be the Lord, who has delivered you out of the hand of the Egyptians and out of the hand of Pharaoh and has delivered the people from under the hand of the Egyptians. 11 Now I know that the Lord is greater than all gods, because in this affair they dealt arrogantly with the people." 12 And Jethro, Moses' father-in-law, brought a burnt offering and sacrifices to God; and Aaron came with all the elders of Israel to eat bread with Moses' father-in-law before God.* ESV

2A. List all the things Jethro said and did in this passage and the implications.

> *Rejoiced and praised God - his testimony.
> *This led to worship (brought sacrifices to Yahweh).
> *The elders ate a meal with Jethro, meaning acceptance.

2B. What did it mean that Jethro brought a burnt offering and sacrifices?

> *He accepted Yahweh as his God – sacrifices were a form of worship.
> *He believed that this would make him right with God, cover his sin, etc.

2C. What is the significance of Aaron and the elders eating with Jethro?
> *Acceptance.
> *Assurance.

Principle #3: Gain Knowledge and Understanding

Exodus 18:13-16   *The next day Moses sat to judge the people, and the people stood around Moses from morning till evening. 14 When Moses' father-in-law saw all that he was doing for the people, he said, "What is this that you are doing for the people? Why do you sit alone, and all the people stand around you from morning till evening?" 15 And Moses said to his father-in-law, "Because the people come to me to inquire of God; 16 when they have a dispute, they come to me and I decide between one person and another, and I make them know the statutes of God and his laws."* ESV

3A. What did Jethro do to gain understanding?

> *He asked questions, because he wanted to know what was going on, and understand the environment.

3B. Did Jethro question the wisdom of anything Moses was doing in this passage?

> *No, just asked questions.

3C. What attitude did Jethro exhibit in obtaining information?

> *Courteous. He was not critical.

3D. What did Moses mean by, "I teach them God's statutes and laws"?

> *Through giving out judgments and decisions based on God's law, Moses was teaching the people the laws of God (rules of life).
> *What was right and what was wrong.
> *NOTE: The Law had not yet been given – Moses was mostly settling disputes.

Principle #4: Delegate, Get Help – You Cannot do it Alone

Exodus 18:17-18   *Moses' father-in-law said to him, "What you are doing is not good. 18 You and the people with you will certainly wear yourselves out, for the thing is too heavy for you. You are not able to do it alone."* ESV

4A. What did Jethro observe Moses doing? What problem did Jethro identify?

> *Trying to do all the work.
> *Not sharing the workload.
> *Not delegating.
> *The leader should not try to do everything.

4B. What was Jethro's attitude in this situation?

> *Jethro was <u>blunt</u>: "You will wear yourself out!"
> *"You will give out. You can't do it alone."
>> *We can't work 10-16 hour days, 6-7 days a week, and expect to be effective. Something will eventually give out, particularly our health and our relationships.

4C. If you are not sure someone is capable, what should you do?

> *Follow their work more closely for a while.
> *Have them run big decisions by you before they implement.
> *Partner them with someone with experience for a while to help them think through decisions.
> *Train them!

Principle #5: Get Attention When Giving Advice

Exodus 18:19a   *Now obey my voice; I will give you advice, and God be with you!* ESV

5A. What three things did Jethro do before he told Moses anything?

      1. _____   *He got Moses' attention ("Listen to me!").
      2. _____   *Told him what he was doing (gave advice).
      3. _____   *Put God in the picture through blessing.

5B. Did Jethro suggest that he would get involved and help Moses?

    *No.
    *He did not offer to do it or become involved in any way.
        *We tend to think we must jump to fix the
        problem rather than let the one responsible do it.

5C. Do you think Jethro should have offered his help?

    *Maybe, but all situations different.
    *Probably not Jethro's place to become involved.

5D. What does "*and God be with you*" do for the advice that will follow?

    *Sets attitude that Jethro is trying to help and calls on God to help Moses.
    *Makes it more difficult for Moses to take the advice in the wrong way.

Principle #6: Understand Your Skills/Calling

Exodus 18:19b-20   *You shall represent the people before God and bring their cases to God, 20 and you shall warn them about the statutes and the laws, and make them know the way in which they must walk and what they must do.* ESV

6A. What could Moses do that the people could not?

> *Speak to God.
> *Be their priest and intermediary before God .
> *Pray – he had the ear of God.

6B. What unique knowledge did Moses possess?

> *How to apply God's ways to life.
> *Moses could do a lot of things well, but he had a special relationship with God that the others did not have!
> *He needed to let the people do the things they could do and he needed to do what he was called to do.
> *That is true for us as well.

6C. What is the significance of the phrase "*teach them the way to live*"?

> *Teach them how to apply the ways of their God to their daily lives.
> *It's not just about the Sabbath!
> *It's not just about following the rules.

Principle #7: Choose (Hire) the Best People

Exodus 18:21a   *Moreover, look for able men from all the people, men who fear God, who are trustworthy and hate a bribe.*   ESV

7A. Summarize what Jethro told Moses to do? Why?

> *Select <u>best</u> men with high character that could do the job.
> *People he could trust to do it and do it right.

7B. List the attributes of the people Jethro told Moses to select.

a.	_____	*Able.
b.	_____	*God-fearing.
c.	_____	*Trustworthy.
d.	_____	*Can't be bribed.

7C. Excluding being "able" what is the nature of the other characteristics?

>***HIGH Character** - People can be trained in work and skills, but it is very difficult to train someone to be of high character (e.g. to be honest!). Start with high character and train the skills. When you have people with good character you can delegate and give authority and responsibility, and be confident they will do it.

7D. What kind of people do some managers hire?

>*People of lesser skills so not a threat to boss.
>   {see next question}
>*Family members or friends.
>*People who owe a favor.
>*People with power, contacts, money or power.
>*Q. Why do some leaders do the opposite of this advice?
>   Most interested in keeping their job.
>   Doing a favor for a friend, family-member, or someone with power.

Principle #8: Span of Control
Exodus 18:21b, 25   *. . . place such men over the people as chiefs of thousands, of hundreds, of fifties, and of tens . . . 25 Moses chose able men out of all Israel and made them heads over the people, chiefs of thousands, of hundreds, of fifties, and of tens.* ESV

8A. How many subordinates should each manager have to supervise?

>*10.

8B. Other than span of control, why is this good advice?

>*Logical.
>*It is fair – treat everyone alike.
>*Allow equal performance evaluations.
>*Creates good will.

> *Allow training good leaders from the ground up.
> *Allow establishment of good personal relationships.

8C. What typically happens when you have 20 people reporting to one supervisor?

> *One cannot manage many more than 10 without losing control.
> *Spread too thin and cannot give adequate time to individuals.
> *Frequently leads to rushed decisions and ultimately bad decisions.

8D. What typically happens when you have only 2 or 3 people reporting to one supervisor?

> *Supervisor may start doing the work because not busy.
> *Supervisor may do work he is not supposed to be doing.
> *May get lazy and not do much work at all.

Principle #9: Authority and Responsibility

Ex 18:22a   *And let them judge the people at all times.* ESV

Note: The ability to judge means they can hold people accountable.

9A. What happens when someone is given the responsibility for a job, but not the authority (can't judge)?

> *Trouble: conflict with others who think they have authority.
> *Job may get done twice.
> *Need: simple organizational hierarchy (chain of command), with different levels of responsibility, that is clear to all concerned.

9B. What happens when someone is given the authority for a job, but not the responsibility?

> *Often the job does not get done, particularly if no one is given responsibility.
> *The one with authority tries to get someone else who does not have the responsibility to do the job.
> *Bad feelings are often created because the conflict of authority vs. responsibility causes suspicion and often open rebellion.

9C. What if someone in authority makes a mistake?

> *Everyone should understand we all make mistakes.
> *Do they learn or keep making the same mistakes?
> *Mistakes (like suffering) help people grow.

Principle #10: Teamwork

Exodus 18:22b   *Every great matter they shall bring to you, but any small matter they shall decide themselves. So it will be easier for you, and they will bear the burden with you.*   ESV

10A. Jethro repeated some of the advice he had already given Moses. What did he repeat?

1. _____
> *Bring Moses the important cases.
> (That is what Moses is called to do.)

2. _____
> *Delegate to others the minor cases.

3. _____
> *Lighten your load – don't try to do it all.

10B. What is the meaning or significance of the phrase, "and they will bear it with you"?

> *Teamwork - You are going to do it *together.*

10C. Why is teamwork important? What are the benefits of good teamwork?

> *Cooperation.
> *Good working relationships.
> *We are in it together.
> *Support for each other.
> *Comradery.

Principle #11: Explain Advice or Decisions

Exodus 18:23   *If you do this, God will direct you, you will be able to endure, and all this people also will go to their place in peace.* ESV

11A. What did Jethro imply should be Moses' first responsibility?

> *To determine that God agrees!
> *It is Moses and God deciding to do it – it's not Jethro.

11B. Why is explaining your advice or decisions a good idea?

> *Cooperation.
> *Understanding.
> *Buy-in.
> *Not demand.

11C. If Jethro hadn't explained the advantages of following his advice, what might have happened?

> *Moses might keep on doing it – not understand what/why.
> *Moses needed to know how to monitor the results for success:
>> *Moses wouldn't be exhausted.
>> *Others would be satisfied.
> *Moses might implement but not take ownership.

Principle #12: Listen

Exodus 18:24   *So Moses listened to the voice of his father-in-law and did all that he had said.*   ESV

12A. Why did Moses implement Jethro's advice?

> *It was good advice.
> *Understood why to do it.
> *Moses wanted the intended result.
> *He was able to determine that it was good advice, partly because Jethro explained his reasoning.

12B. How difficult is it to learn the art of listening?

> *Not easy.

12C. How did Jethro make it a little easier for Moses to listen?

> *He inserted God and gave Moses a blessing [see Ex 18:19].

Implications and Observations

Why do you suppose God sent Jethro to Moses with this advice? Moses' situation was unique. He was leading more than 2 million people, families, tribes, and their equipment in a wilderness area that provided little comfort. This was not an organized army of soldiers who had been trained and prepared. These were scared, disorganized individuals and groups of all ages who had no idea what they were doing or what was going to happen to them.

All they had was Moses – and God!

What did Moses know about leading this many people? Very little! This was as new and frightening to him as it was to the people he was leading. Remember, Moses didn't want to do this in the first place. Originally he had all kinds of excuses why he could not go to Pharaoh and demand that Pharaoh "let his people go."

God used Jethro to give Moses a quick course in leadership, delegation, and organization. If this teaching and advice by Jethro had <u>not</u> occurred, Moses would have had much more difficulty leading Israel around the wilderness.

In some ways Moses' job was an impossible nightmare. Bringing organization and hierarchy to the mass exodus was a major step in making it possible for Israel to move through the wilderness from one location to another.

Large families survive through organization, delegation, and cooperation. Mom and Dad don't do all the work; the children are given responsibilities and authority to accomplish certain areas of work. Mom and Dad get involved only when necessary or when the kids lack the skills or ability.

APPLICATION

1. Do you know anyone who needs leadership advice? How could you help?

2. Are you trying to do everything? Do you need to delegate to others? Who could help you at work, home, your church . . . ?

3. How are you at taking, accepting, and evaluating advice? Do you listen well? Do you <u>really</u> listen well?

4. Who is your "Jethro"? Are you listening? Why? Why not?

5. Do you need to be a Jethro to someone? Who?

Manoah & Wife
parents of Samson
NOTE: Manoah's wife is never named,
but referred to only as "his wife" or the "woman."

**Occurrences of "Manoah/wife/woman"
in Judges 13:** 16/10/5

Themes: The Angel of the Lord; a Nazirite Vow

Scripture: **Judges 13:1-24**   Birth of Samson, the Last Judge

And the people of Israel again did what was evil in the sight of the Lord, so the Lord gave them into the hand of the Philistines for forty years. 2 There was a certain man of Zorah, of the tribe of the Danites, whose name was Manoah. And his wife was barren and had no children. 3 And the angel of the Lord appeared to the woman and said to her, "Behold, you are barren and have not borne children, but you shall conceive and bear a son. 4 Therefore be careful and drink no wine or strong drink, and eat nothing unclean, 5 for behold, you shall conceive and bear a son. No razor shall come upon his head, for the child shall be a Nazirite to God from the womb, and he shall begin to save Israel from the hand of the Philistines." 6 Then the woman came and told her husband, "A man of God came to me, and his appearance was like the appearance of the angel of God, very awesome. I did not ask him where he was from, and he did not tell me his name, 7 but he said to me, 'Behold, you shall conceive and bear a son. So then drink no wine or strong drink, and eat nothing unclean, for the child shall be a Nazirite to God from the womb to the day of his death.'"

8 Then Manoah prayed to the Lord and said, "O Lord, please let the man of God whom you sent come again to us and teach us what we are to do with the child who will be born." 9 And God listened to the

voice of Manoah, and the angel of God came again to the woman as she sat in the field. But Manoah her husband was not with her. 10 So the woman ran quickly and told her husband, "Behold, the man who came to me the other day has appeared to me." 11 And Manoah arose and went after his wife and came to the man and said to him, "Are you the man who spoke to this woman?" And he said, "I am." 12 And Manoah said, "Now when your words come true, what is to be the child's manner of life, and what is his mission?" 13 And the angel of the Lord said to Manoah, "Of all that I said to the woman let her be careful. 14 She may not eat of anything that comes from the vine, neither let her drink wine or strong drink, or eat any unclean thing. All that I commanded her let her observe."

15 Manoah said to the angel of the Lord, "Please let us detain you and prepare a young goat for you." 16 And the angel of the Lord said to Manoah, "If you detain me, I will not eat of your food. But if you prepare a burnt offering, then offer it to the Lord." (For Manoah did not know that he was the angel of the Lord.) 17 And Manoah said to the angel of the Lord, "What is your name, so that, when your words come true, we may honor you?" 18 And the angel of the Lord said to him, "Why do you ask my name, seeing it is wonderful?" 19 So Manoah took the young goat with the grain offering, and offered it on the rock to the Lord, to the one who works wonders, and Manoah and his wife were watching. 20 And when the flame went up toward heaven from the altar, the angel of the Lord went up in the flame of the altar. Now Manoah and his wife were watching, and they fell on their faces to the ground.

21 The angel of the Lord appeared no more to Manoah and to his wife. Then Manoah knew that he was the angel of the Lord. 22 And Manoah said to his wife, "We shall surely die, for we have seen God." 23 But his wife said to him, "If the Lord had meant to kill us, he would not have accepted a burnt offering and a grain offering at our hands, or shown us all these things, or now announced to us such things as these." 24 And the woman bore a son and called his name Samson. And the young man grew, and the Lord blessed him. ESV

Context

Chapter 13 of Judges describes the circumstances leading up to the birth of Samson, who was probably the last judge in Israel. We are told the conflicting information that Manoah and his wife would be the parents of Samson and that she was unable to conceive. But just as on several other occasions, God had a plan for the barren woman. There had been a number of different and special judges in Israel's history and Samson was the last. So it may be fitting that the last judge came into the world under some rather special circumstances, beginning with his parents.

What Do We Know?

Although Manoah seemed confused by the identity of the Angel of the Lord for most of the story, he finally figured it out in the end when he said, *"We shall surely die, for we have seen God!"* The reader is told early in the chapter that the Angel of the Lord visited Manoah's wife. The wife apparently understood who she had encountered because when she reported the visitation to her husband she referred to the visitor as *"A man of God . . . His appearance was like the appearance of the angel of God, very awesome."* ESV

As a contrast to the story of Sarah and Abraham and the birth of Isaac, Manoah and his wife appear to have no doubt regarding the birth of the child. Of course, Abraham and Sarah had a very long wait before their birth, which gave them more time and more reason to become doubtful.

We should note that Manoah's wife reported that she did not know the name of the man of God, and one of the questions that Manoah asked when he met the man was, "What is your name?" It's interesting that the visitor did not answer that question.

The angel said that the child was to be a *Nazirite* from birth.

The Nazirite Vow

The vow of the Nazirite is defined in Numbers 6:1-21. To summarize, it was usually a voluntary and very personal vow for a temporary period of time for the purpose of dedicated service to God. Tradition indicates that most vows were for 30, 60, or 90 to 100 days. The Bible reports only three instances of a man being a Nazirite for life: Samuel, John the Baptist, and Samson. The nature of this vow is described in Numbers 6:2 where it says the Nazirite "separates himself to the Lord." The word "separates" is *consecrates* in other translations.

This consecration committed the Nazirite to follow some very specific rules, including:

(1) abstain from wine and other grape drinks,
(2) refrain from cutting the hair during the period of the vow, and
(3) avoid contact with the dead, including family members.

Because these requirements produced visible signs, a Nazirite vow was public knowledge. The decision to be a Nazirite was not limited to special people or circumstances; anyone could take the vow.

The Nazirite typically made two commitments. The first was to follow all the rules and requirements specified in the Law. The Nazirite dedicated himself to following every requirement and if by intention or accident he violated one of the rules, his consecrated time started over.

Secondly, the Nazirite usually committed himself to a special service or abstinence. The Nazitite would not be released from his vow until this special service was fully completed. Often the man under a vow would separate himself from family and normal activities in order to concentrate totally on completing the vow and focusing on the Lord.

When the specified period of time was over and the service had been completed, the Nazirite would go to the priest to be released from the vow. [9A (Nelson's); 9B (ISBE)]

Implications and Observations

Israel's time of the judges might be described as a period of no leadership. The people of Israel failed to place their trust in God as their leader and refused to stay committed to those leaders God raised up to free them from the oppression brought on by their apostasy. Therefore, they lived in a cycle that was either going from good to bad, or from bad to good. This life cycle can be outlined as follows:

PEACE:	Living at peace, seeking the Lord.
APOSTASY:	Rebellion, idolatry, and apostasy.
JUDGMENT:	God's judgment on Israel in the form of oppression by other nations or Canaanite peoples.
PLEADING:	Pleading for help and deliverance.
LEADER:	God raising up a leader.
REPENTANCE:	The people turn from their wicked ways.
RESTORATION:	Restoration by God and living in peace for a period of time.

The author uses several repeated phrases to illustrate the cycle outlined above:

Judges 3:11   "*the land had rest*" for forty years.
Judges 13:1a   They "*did what was evil in the sight of the Lord.*"
Judges 13:1b   "*the Lord gave them into*" the hand.]
                       [or 10:7 says: He "*sold them into the . . .*"]
Judges 17:6   In those days "*there was no king in Israel.*
                       "*Everyone did what was right in his own eyes.*"

Israel's fundamental problem was that they never completed the task of owning the land and driving out the evil Canaanite influence as God had commanded. Because of this, Israel was attracted to the pagan gods and goddesses and fell into and out of idolatry, rather than focusing continually and completely on the kingship of their God.

Another interesting fact in the story of this judge was that there is no indication that the people actually cried out to the Lord to be saved or delivered. However, God sent a judge to lead them against the Philistine oppression.

Discussion Questions

A. GENERAL

A1. Judges 13:1 says Israel again, *"did what was evil in the sight of the Lord."* What does this mean? What was Israel doing?

> *Israel was in the cycle of peace, sin, judgment, pleading for help, God raising up a Judge, and repentance.
> *It was a cycle that was continually repeated.
> *Israel had no spiritual leadership; therefore rather than follow God's direction, they did what they wanted to do.
> *They continually became complacent and spiritually lazy which led to heresy, apostasy, idolatry, etc.
> *They had many pagan gods to choose from because they had never rid the land of the Cannanites.
> *This is the point in the cycle between Peace and Apostasy. They had been rescued by the judge and were at peace for some period of time, but then they deteriorated into sin again, ignored God, and began to do evil again.

A2. The passage goes on to say that *"the Lord gave them into the hand of the Philistines."* Why would God do such a thing? What part of the cycle is this?

> *This is the next step in the cycle.
> *They were ignoring the Lord, living in sin (not "fear").
> *After some time the Lord would execute judgment by handing them over to the Philistines.
> *PURPOSE: so that eventually they would come back to the Lord, pleading for His mercy and help.

>> Q. How does this judgment differ from the story of Sodom and Gomorrah?
>> *S&G: God destroyed the cities directly.
>> *Samson: God allowed Philistines to oppress the people.

LEADER: If you have time, you might ask the group whether they think God runs out of patience or is simply allowing time for repentance. And, when they do not repent, He executes judgment.

B. THE ANGEL OF THE LORD

B1. Who was "The Angel of the Lord" (13:3)? Explain.

*God; Jesus; Special Angel of God.

*ANGEL OF THE LORD: A mysterious messenger of God, sometimes described as the Lord Himself (Gen 16:10-13; Ex 3:2-6; 23:20; Judg 6:11-18), but at other times as one sent by God. The Lord used this messenger to appear to human beings who otherwise would not be able to see Him and live (Ex 33:20). The Angel of the Lord performed actions associated with God, such as revelation, deliverance, and destruction; but he can be spoken of as distinct from God (2 Sam 24:16; Zech 1:12). This special relationship is a mystery similar to that between Jesus and God in the New Testament. [10 (Nelson's)]

*ANGEL OF THE LORD: Gen 16:7, etc. The special form in which God manifested Himself to man, and hence Christ's visible form before the incarnation. Compare Acts 7:30-38, with the corresponding Old Testament history; and Gen 18:1, 13, 14, 33, and Gen 19:1). [11 (Smith's)]

B2. In the culture of that day the husband ruled the family, yet on both visits, the angel appeared first to Manoah's wife and did not speak to Manoah at all on the first visit. Why? Is this curious?

*All applied to wife: Manoah was not asked to do anything.
*Maybe God did not trust Manoah to understand or obey.
*Later on it appears that Manoah's faith may not have been very strong so maybe the angel appeared to wife because of concern that Manoah would not understand. He didn't actually recognize the Angel of the Lord until the angel ascended in the fire while the wife seemed to understand the situation.

B3. When Manoah met with the angel, he asked, *"Are You the man who spoke to this woman?"* Would this have been your first question? If not, what would you have asked first?

> *Are you sent from God? If so, prove it.
> *Why are you here? What do I have to know or do?
> *Manoah's question seems "dull" because his wife had already identified the visitor.

B4. What did Manoah or his wife learn on the second visit from the angel that they did not know from the first visit?

> *Not much!
> *Only thing: wife not to eat anything from the grapevine.
> *Maybe understand that wife is participating in the vow.
>
> *Q. If only the wife is participating, why?
> *Ans: Maybe Manoah was jealous that the angel met with his wife rather than him – it is not clear from text.

B5. Since there was very little new information in the second visit from the angel, why did the angel come back?

> *The only logical reason seems to be to confirm the instructions for wife to Manoah; verify wife's story.
> *The angel did not answer anything about what to teach or how to raise the child as Manoah asked in his prayer.
> *Maybe Manoah was not easily convinced by wife's story
> *If Manoah was a man of weak faith, this visit might encourage his faith/obedience.
> *Remember, nothing was required of Manoah – only his wife.

B6. Why do you think it took so long for Manoah to recognize the Angel of the Lord?

*He might have been spiritually dull. Dullness may be the reason that the angel appeared to wife and not to Manoah.
*He was being cautious, since his position as head of the family was not acknowledged by angel.

B7. Why do you think the Angel of the Lord chose to ascend in the flame of the fire?

*Dramatic affect – convince Manoah of identity.
*It was the flame of a burnt offering – not just a normal fire but an act of worship.
*Demonstrate approval of the sacrifice (act of worship).

C. NAZIRITE VOW

C1. How does Samson's Nazirite vow differ from most Nazirite vows? A normal vow would involve abstaining from fermented drink, refraining from cutting hair, and avoiding a corpse.

*Most are made by the individual, not commanded by God.
*Most are temporary for relatively short periods of time.
*Not only was this one declared prior to birth, but restrictions applied to mother during pregnancy.

C2. What is interesting or curious about verse 13:4b?
"Therefore be careful and drink no wine or strong drink, and eat nothing unclean." ESV

*NOTE: this is not a requirement in Nu 6 for a Nazirite.
*It is a test of obedience? Maybe Manoah and wife were not keeping the dietary laws?
*This is another hint of the spiritual condition of Manoah's family.
*Emphasis on the spiritual nature surrounding birth.

NOTE: The instruction not to eat anything unclean would have been true for all of Israel. Therefore, it might be an indication that Manoah and his wife were not careful in following the law, or that their level of spiritual holiness was somewhat lacking.

C3. Is there any significance to the fact that the Angel of the Lord told the mother that her son would be a Nazirite from birth?

*EXTRAORDINARY: this is not a typical Nazirite vow! It put responsibility directly on the mother (parents) from birth until the child was old enough to understand.
*He would be prepared from birth for the Nazirite commitment but also to lead his people.
*This was to be a serious consecration of this child because his calling was known from birth.
*It put much greater responsibility on parents.

C4. Why do you think it says Samson will "*begin*" to save Israel?

*He failed as a Nazirite.
*He failed to save/restore Israel.
*Q. What did Samson actually accomplish?
    Ans: Very little!

*SAMSON:
A hero of Israel known for his great physical strength as well as his moral weakness. Samson was a person with great potential who fell short because of his sin and disobedience. Mighty in physical strength, he was weak in resisting temptation. His life is a clear warning against the dangers of self-indulgence and lack of discipline. Samson's life was marred by his weakness for pagan women. As soon as he became of age, he fell in love with one of the daughters of the Philistines. He insisted on marrying her, in spite of his parents' objection (Judg 14:1-4). This was against God's law, which forbade intermarriage of the Israelites among the women of Canaan. On another occasion he was almost captured by the Philistines while he was visiting a prostitute in the city of Gaza. [12 (Nelson's)]

The story about Samson killing the lion and later eating the honey he found in its carcass (vv. 5-9) illustrates both his heroic strength and his disregard of the Nazirite prohibition against contact with dead bodies. He violated his vows again by having a wedding "feast" at which there was heavy drinking.

HAIR: he finally divulged the secret of his strength: the Nazirite vow prohibiting the cutting of his hair. While he was sleeping his hair was shorn, and "his strength left him." The Philistines seized him, gouged out his eyes, and forced him to perform the humiliating task of grinding in the prison.[13] (ISBE)

D. MANOAH'S PRAYER

D1. Manoah prayed in 13:8. What was the purpose of the prayer? Is this what you would have prayed?
Judges 13:8   *Then Manoah prayed to the Lord and said, "O Lord, please let the man of God whom you sent come again to us and teach us what we are to do with the child who will be born." ESV*

> *Verification of wife's story.
> *Clarification that she got it correct.
> *Knowledge and understanding of what they are to do.
> *Help in carrying out their responsibilities.

D2. Was this a normal parental prayer? What might it mean or signify?

> *VERIFY: Manoah had only the word of his wife and he wanted first-hand verification.
> *In Judges 13:6 the wife seemed confused as to who visited her.
> *Might indicate concern by Manoah to be proper parent - maybe he felt overwhelmed by the responsibility.
> *Note, he prayed to be "taught." He may have felt inadequate. Maybe he was just being cautious.

D3. What is interesting about who prayed and God's response?

> *Manoah prayed but he was not the one the angel
> appeared to, nor was he requested to do anything.
> *Q. To whom did God give the instruction?
> > First visit: the instructions were only given to wife.
> > Second visit: the wife was told to do all the angel said.
> *The angel gave no instructions to Manoah, even when
> questioned by Manoah.
> *NOTE: Manoah's prayer for "teaching" was not answered,
> although the angel returned for a second visit.

E. ANGEL'S NAME

E1. Why would Manoah and his wife be so concerned about
knowing the name of the visitor?

> *The name often reflected the identity, authority, or
> nature of the person.
> *If it were God, it would have been possible to learn the
> nature of God from the name.
> *Maybe be blessed by God.

E2. Was there significance in the angel telling them that his name
was "wonderful"? [or beyond understanding]

> *Manoah would not have understood, regardless.
> *This is the same word used in Isaiah 9:6.
> Isa 9:6   *to us a child is born, to us a son is given; and the government
> shall be upon his shoulder, and his name shall be called Wonderful
> Counselor, Mighty God, Everlasting Father, Prince of Peace.* ESV
>
> *NOTE: May imply this is the pre-incarnate Jesus?
>
> *Q. Was the angel's statement to Manoah a hint of what
> God thought of Manoah?   Ans: Maybe => Dull!

E3. Why do you think the angel ignored the question of His name?

> *It was the Angel of the Lord.
> *God did not want Manoah and his wife to lose focus.
> *Wanted to focus on instruction to wife.
> *If was pre-incarnate Jesus, then might create commotion not related to the real and present assignment for wife.

F. APPLICATION

F1. Samson's Nazirite vow separated him from normal society in an effort to keep him focused on God. How do <u>you</u> try to keep focused on God/Jesus? How difficult is it to keep the world's values from overcoming your value system? How do you try to be holy (set apart)? What do you do to "keep your eyes on Jesus"?

> ***LEADER:** This is an important question. If your group is reluctant to respond, you might ask:
>
> > *Do you have a regular quiet time?
> >
> > *Do you listen regularly to worship music?
> >
> > *Do you have a regular prayer time?

F2. Have you ever failed or been slow to recognize God or His work in either your life, or in the life of your family? If so,

(1) Are you really looking?

(2) Are you ever in a state of awareness?

(3) Are you asking?

F3. What could you do in <u>your</u> life to sharpen your awareness?

   *Prayer; fasting; personal worship.

F4. Have you ever set aside a time of fasting in order to focus on God? Have you ever undertaken a time of intense Bible study? Explain.

Hathach
a messenger for Esther

Occurrences of "Hathach" in the Bible: 5

Themes: Loyalty; Trustworthiness; God's Providence

Scripture

Esther 3:13   Decree to Annihilate the Jews
Letters were sent by couriers to all the king's provinces with instruction to destroy, to kill, and to annihilate all Jews, young and old, women and children, in one day, the thirteenth day of the twelfth month, which is the month of Adar, and to plunder their goods. ESV

Esther 4:1-17   Esther Agrees to Help the Jews
When Mordecai learned all that had been done, Mordecai tore his clothes and put on sackcloth and ashes, and went out into the midst of the city, and he cried out with a loud and bitter cry. 2 He went up to the entrance of the king's gate, for no one was allowed to enter the king's gate clothed in sackcloth. 3 And in every province, wherever the king's command and his decree reached, there was great mourning among the Jews, with fasting and weeping and lamenting, and many of them lay in sackcloth and ashes.

4 When Esther's young women and her eunuchs came and told her, the queen was deeply distressed. She sent garments to clothe Mordecai, so that he might take off his sackcloth, but he would not accept them. 5 Then Esther called for Hathach, one of the king's eunuchs, who had been appointed to attend her, and ordered him to go to Mordecai to learn what this was and why it was. 6 Hathach went out to Mordecai in the open square of the city in front of the king's gate, 7 and Mordecai told him all that had happened to him, and the exact sum of money that Haman had promised to pay into the king's treasuries for the destruction of the Jews. 8 Mordecai also gave him a copy of the written decree issued in Susa for their destruction, that he might show it to Esther and explain it to her and command her to go to the king to beg his favor and plead with him on behalf of her people. 9 And Hathach went and told Esther what Mordecai had said. 10 Then Esther spoke to Hathach and commanded him to go to Mordecai and say, 11 "All the king's servants and the people of the king's provinces know that if any man or woman goes to the king inside the inner court without being called, there is but one law—to be put to death, except the one to whom the king holds out the golden scepter so that he may live. But as for me, I have not been called to come in to the king these thirty days."

12 And they told Mordecai what Esther had said. 13 Then Mordecai told them to reply to Esther, "Do not think to yourself that in the king's palace you will escape any more than all the other Jews. 14 For if you keep silent at this time, relief and deliverance will rise for the Jews from another place, but you and your father's house will perish. And who knows whether you have not come to the kingdom for such a time as this?" 15 Then Esther told them to reply to Mordecai, 16 "Go, gather all the Jews to be found in Susa, and hold a fast on my behalf, and do not eat or drink for three days, night or day. I and my young women will also fast as you do. Then I will go to the king, though it is against the law, and if I perish, I perish." 17 Mordecai then went away and did everything as Esther had ordered him. ESV

The Context

The purpose of the book of Esther is to record the origin of the festival of Purim and to keep alive the memory of the story of Queen Esther and the man Mordecai. In Chapter 1 we learn the details of why Queen Vashti was deposed. She was ordered to appear before king Xerxes but she refused. Bad choice! In Chapter 2 the king decided he needed to replace Vashti and Esther was chosen. Esther was Jewish but upon Mordecai's advice, had chosen not to reveal her nationality.

Mordecai overheard a plot to kill the king and reported what he heard to Queen Esther. She told the king, giving credit to Mordecai as the source of the information. Sometime later the king honored Haman, one of his officials, and elevated him above all the other nobles, declaring that all should bow before Haman. Mordecai refused, which angered Haman. In fact, he was "enraged." This led Haman to suggest to the king that "the people of Mordecai" (all the Jews) were not obeying the king's command and it would be in the king's best interest to destroy them. To further encourage the king, Haman promised to put 10,000 talents of silver in the royal treasury. The king said, "Keep the money," and told Haman to do with the people as he chose. The king did not even ask Haman to identify the people he wished to destroy.

What Do We Know?

Haman prepared a decree in the first month of the year declaring that all the Jewish people were to be annihilated on the 13th day of the twelfth month. The destruction was to occur on a single day and would include women and children. The goods and possessions of the Jews were to be plundered.

Thus, for 11 months the Jewish people had a death sentence hanging over their heads and waited with great fear and trepidation for the designated day of their annihilation. When Mordecai learned about the decree, he put on sackcloth and ashes and went into the city wailing loudly and bitterly (4:1).

Implications and Observations

It is interesting to note that when Esther was being considered for the position of the new queen, Mordecai *forbade* her to reveal her nationality (2:10; 2:20). The fact that this was mentioned twice probably means that the author thought it was significant to the story.

Mordecai had helped raise Esther as a child and would certainly have felt some parental responsibility for her. Given the fact the

Jews were living as exiles in a foreign country he probably thought that keeping her nationality secret was either an advantage in being considered for the position of queen, or that she might actually be in danger if her nationality was known.

This "secret" is not a factor in the story but it does hang over the proceedings as they develop. The thought that the king might find out her ethnic background was always a possibility. Likewise, if Haman found out she was Jewish he might use the information against her or use it as leverage to gain some advantage with the king.

But finally Queen Esther revealed her nationality to the king in Haman's presence (7.3). The king had no concern about Esther's nationality and proceeded to execute Haman because of his scheme to annihilate Esther's people. The king seemed to make this decision without much thought. Haman apparently tricked him, Esther was in the king's good graces, and so the king ordered the evil Haman to hang on the gallows he had built for Mordecai. Done!

Discussion Questions:

A. GENERAL

A1. Who exactly was to be killed (3:13)?

> *All the Jewish people - everyone, including women and children.

A2. What started all this terrible business (see 3:5)?

> *Mordecai was (1) not bowing down, and (2) not paying the king and Haman homage.

A3. In 3:7-11 what did Haman tell the king about the Jews?

> *Identified as <u>one</u> ethnic group that did not obey, but not identified as Hebrews, Jews, or an entire people group.
> *They were scattered throughout all the provinces.
> *They were living in isolation.
> *They had not been integrated into the culture.
> *Their laws were different.
> *They did not obey the king's laws.
> *Best not to tolerate them - they would cause trouble.

A4. In 3:10-11, what did the king find out about the people to be destroyed before giving his approval?

> *Absolutely nothing.

> *Q. How does this strike you? What does it say about the king? Ans: <u>Self-absorbed; no concern about human life.</u>

> *Q. Can you even imagine such a callous, uncaring response?

A5. What does it mean that Mordecai and many Jews in the nation "put on sackcloth and ashes"?

> *Sign of grief . . . tearing clothes was sign of great distress sackcloth: A rough, coarse cloth, or a baglike garment made of this cloth and worn as a symbol of mourning or repentance. Often used to symbolize certain actions. In the case of mourning, either over a death (Gen 37:34; Joel 1:8) or another calamity (Est 4:1-4; Job 16:15), the Israelites showed their grief by wearing sackcloth and ashes. Sackcloth was often worn by prophets, perhaps to show their own brokenness in the face of their terrible messages of judgment and doom (Isa 20:2; Rev 11:3). Sackcloth was most commonly used as an article of clothing.[14 (Nelson's)]

A6. Can you think of another situation in Scripture when someone put on sackcloth and ashes?

*Jacob	Gen 37:34
*Job	Job 16:15
*David	Ps 35:13
*Daniel	Dan 9:3
*Ninevites	Jonah 3:5
*Two Witnesses	Rev 11:3

*Mentioned 13 times in books of Isaiah and Jeremiah

A7. Queen Esther heard the news from her servants and was overcome with fear. Why do you think Esther reacted in this way?

*She was a Jew and understood the significance.
*NOTE: She may not have believed that the king would save her.

A8. In 4:4 Esther sent clothes to Mordecai so he would take off his sackcloth. Do Esther's actions make sense? Why would she do this?

*Mordecai surely had other clothes he could wear.
*She was showing support, but this would change the message Mordecai wanted to convey.
*She was afraid for Mordecai and for herself and wanted Mordecai to stop.

A9. Do you think Esther wanted Mordecai to stop his public display?

*Maybe.
*She may have feared the timetable would be advanced if the Jews spoke out.

A10. Esther sent Hathach on a mission (4:5). What did Esther want Hathach to do? Why would Esther do this? The servants and eunuchs had already reported the news to Esther.

> *Sent him to Mordecai.
> *Find out what Mordecai was doing and why?
> *Esther wanted to verify the news.
> *Esther wanted more details.
> *Esther didn't totally trust news and wanted a firsthand account from a trusted messenger.
> *Wanted Mordecai to know she knew what was going on.
> *Servants reported what Mordecai was doing but not why.

A11. Why is Hathach necessary? Why didn't Mordecai visit Esther or Esther visit Mordecai?

> *Esther would not have been allowed out – probably living in protected harem quarters.
> *Mordecai had on sackcloth and would not have been allowed through the gate.

A12. What did Mordecai tell Hathach (4:7) and how would Mordecai know all this information, particularly the amount that Haman had pledged to the treasury?

> *". . . all that had happened" (4.7)
> *Including the exact amount Haman was going to pay to the King to annihilate the Jews.
> *Still very well-respected with friends in high places.
> Esther 2:21-23 *In those days, as Mordecai was sitting at the king's gate, Bigthan and Teresh, two of the king's eunuchs, who guarded the threshold, became angry and sought to lay hands on King Ahasuerus. 22 And this came to the knowledge of Mordecai, and he told it to Queen Esther, and Esther told the king in the name of Mordecai. 23 When the affair was investigated and found to be so, the men were both hanged on the gallows. And it was recorded in the book of the chronicles in the presence of the king.* ESV

A13. Why do you think Haman thought it was necessary to offer money to the king?

> *Bribe.
> *Wanted king to know how important it was to him.
> *Money might sway him to agree.
> *It didn't cost the king anything.

A14. List everything you know about Hathach.

> *One of the king's eunuchs.
> *Assigned to Esther.
> *Worked for the king.

A15. Why would Hathach have to explain the written decree to Esther (4:8)?

> *Maybe Esther could not read – or could not read in the language the decree was printed.
> *Maybe Esther was not very savvy (or Mordecai may not know if Esther was savvy enough).
> *Hearing the words spoken can have stronger impact than just reading silently.
> *Most historians think Esther was a teenager, about 14 years old.

A16. Do you find it odd that the king had not seen Esther for 30 days? What might that mean?

> *Esther may have been one of many women visited on some rotational basis.
> *The king and Esther were not getting along well.
> *The king had lost his desire for Esther.

*The king has been very busy with matters of state and not paid much attention to harem.

*Q. Would you say Esther is being treated like a queen or a concubine?   Ans: More like a concubine.

A17. Why do you suppose Haman wanted to destroy the entire Jewish nation?

*Satan.
*Unlikely to be because Mordecai would not bow down.
*Hatred of the Jews.
*NOTE 3:10: *So the king took his signet ring from his hand and gave it to Haman the Agagite, the son of Hammedatha, the enemy of the Jews.* ESV
*A signet ring allows one to seal official documents, therefore, Haman was being given the power and authority of the king. This indicates incredible trust in Haman!
*Pride: self-importance and wanted to elevate self.

A18. What is the meaning of 4:14 where Mordecai advises Esther not to keep silent?

Esther 4:14   *For if you keep silent at this time, relief and deliverance will rise for the Jews from another place, but you and your father's house will perish. And who knows whether you have not come to the kingdom for such a time as this?* ESV
*If Esther were not the instrument to save the Jewish nation, then it would be someone else.
*But if she doesn't help at this time, her family will be destroyed by Haman's plan.
*Maybe Esther was actually God's plan for saving the Jews.

A19. What is the life lesson(s) here?

> *God does not need us to accomplish His plans.
> *If God has called us to be part of His plans, we must
> think seriously how we should respond.

A20. There is a saying, "If you are not part of the solution, then you are part of the problem." Does this apply here?

> *This is what Mordecai said in 4:14, but in a different way.
> *Mordecai is suggesting that Esther may be the one God
> has chosen to fix the problem.

A21. Esther sent very specific instructions to Mordecai:
>   a) Gather all the Jews in Susa.
>   b) Fast for "me" (Esther).
>   c) Do not eat or drink for 3 days (day or night).
What does it mean that Esther requested they fast for her?

> *Fast (and pray) that she will have the courage to break the
> law and be successful in her plan.

A22. What did Esther say she would do and what does this say about her and her maids?

> WOULD DO
> *I (Esther) and my maids will fast as you do.
> *After 3 days I (Esther) will go to the king.
> MAIDS
> *Jews or maybe converts.
> *Very trustworthy.
> *It might be easy for word to get back to king about
> what they are doing.

A23. How important is Hathach in all this activity?

> *If discovered delivering messages, likely put to death or at least jailed.
> *If Hathach was caught, then both Mordecai and Esther would be implicated and in danger.

B. APPLICATION

B1. Are you a good messenger? Can you be trusted to get the story right?

B2. Can you imagine something in your life when you might consider "going against the law," like Esther in this story?

B3. Do you have something serious in your life for which you need to fast and pray? When you have a big challenge or difficulty in your life what is the first thing you think about doing? Is fasting on your list?

B4. Do you have a Mordecai in your life? Do you need one?

B5. Have you ever accepted or refused God's calling? How did that work out? Would a Mordecai have been helpful?

Transformation Road Map

Primary Takeaways

1: God can use ordinary people of faith and simple resources to accomplish extraordinary purposes.

2: Wisdom and guidance can come from unexpected sources. We should be humble enough to listen, learn, and implement godly advice regardless of its origin.

3: Genuine faith involves trusting God's promises and guidance, even in the face of uncertainty or extraordinary circumstances.

4: Faithful service and obedience in seemingly small roles can be instrumental in God's larger plan for His people.

Free PDF

MAKE WISE DECISIONS

[Get the ebook version for 99 cents]

Consequences Shape Lives.

This book discusses the nature of decisions and explores eight essential questions to make better decisions.

You are a few decisions away from transforming your life. You can make better decisions! This resource has sections on what makes a poor decision, questions to ask yourself, traps to avoid, short and sweet decisions, the wise decision framework, and twenty ways to be wise. It also has a handy decision-making checklist. (12 pages)

Free PDF: https://getwisdompublishing.com/resource-registration/

Kindle ebook for 99 cents: https://www.amazon.com/dp/B0FG8NC53J

Ebook

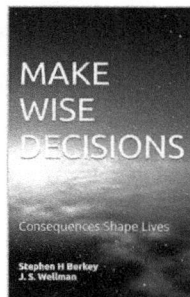
MAKE WISE DECISIONS
Consequences Shape Lives
Stephen H Berkey
J. S. Wellman

Free PDF

Ten Steps to Wise Choices

Timeless Wisdom. Practical Tools. Lasting Impact.

Free PDF
Life Improvement Principles
[Get the ebook version for 99 cents]

You can live your best life!

Welcome to a journey of discovery! In case you have forgotten, your actions have consequences. Unlock your potential! This book (60+ pages) provides the overview of all our strategies and wisdom principles to live your best life. You *can* transform your life! Get your wisdom-based roadmap to a better life and unlock all the possibilities for growth and success.

FreePDF: https://getwisdompublishing.com/resource-registration/

Kindle ebook for 99 cents:
https://www.amazon.com/dp/B0FG883KZM

Ebook

Free PDF

Make it your life goal to be the best you can be!

Discover Wisdom and live the life you deserve.

Next Steps!

Continue Studying the *OBSCURE* Series
The *OBSCURE* Bible Study Series
https://www.amazon.com/dp/B08T7TL1B1

Be Challenged by the Jesus Follower Series
The Jesus Follower Bible Study Series
https://www.amazon.com/dp/B0DHP39P5J

Tackle Wisdom-Driven Life Change
Apply Biblical Wisdom to Live Your Best Life!
"Effective Life Change"
https://www.amazon.com/dp/1952359732

Know What You Should Pray
Personal Daily Prayer Guide
https://www.amazon.com/What-Should-Pray-Personal-Journal/dp/1952359260/

Decide to be the Very Best You Can Be
The Life Planning Series
https://www.amazon.com/dp/B09TH9SYC4

You Can Help:
SOCIAL MEDIA: Mention The *OBSCURE* Bible Study Series on your social platforms. Include the hashtag #obscurebiblestudy so we are aware of your post.

FRIENDS: Recommend *OBSCURE* to your family, friends, small group, Sunday School class leaders, or your church.

REVIEW: Please give us your honest review at
https://www.amazon.com/dp/173440941X

The *OBSCURE* Bible Study Series

Continue your journey through the hidden wisdom of Scripture with the OBSCURE Series.

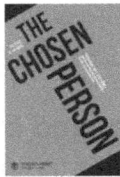

Blasphemy, Grace, Quarrels & Reconciliation: The lives of first-century disciples.
This book presents Joseph of Arimathea, Joanna, Ananias, Hymenaeus, and Cornelius (a centurion). It illustrates the nature and challenges of life as a first-century disciple.

The Beginning and the End: From creation to eternity.
This book has four lessons from Genesis and four from Revelation covering creation, rebellion, grace, worship, and eternity. God is leading us to worship in the Throne Room.

God at the Center: He is sovereign and I am not.
This book examines the virgin birth, worship, prayer, the sovereignty of God, compromise, and trust. God is at the center of all these stories. He is at the center of our lives.

Women of Courage: God did some serious business with these women.
This book examines the lives of Jael, Rizpah, the woman of Tekoa, Tabitha, Shiphrah, and Lydia. These women exhibit great courage and faithfulness. God used them in amazing ways.

The Beginning of Wisdom: Your personal character counts.
In this book we find courage, loyalty, thankfulness, love, forgiveness, and humility. Personal character counts. Decisions have consequences. Wisdom will help us stand firm in our faith.

Miracles & Rebellion: The good, the bad, and the indifferent.
God hates sin and loves to heal the faithful. The rebellion of Korah, Haman, and Alexander compare to the healing stories of Aeneas, a slave girl, and the crippled man at Lystra.

The Chosen People: There is a remnant.
This book concentrates mostly on Israel in the Old Testament, but also covers some interesting subjects as Lucifer, Michael the archangel, and Job's wife.

The Chosen Person: Keep your eyes on Jesus.
The focus is on Jesus and the superiority of Christ. We investigate Melchizedek, the disciples on the road to Emmaus, Nicodemus, and the criminal on the cross.

WEBSITE: http://getwisdompublishing.com/products/
AMAZON: www.amazon.com/author/stephenhberkey

Jesus Follower Bible Study Series

The Jesus Follower Bible Study Series will provide you with a complete description of the nature, characteristics, obligations, commitments, and responsibilities of a true Jesus follower.

Go to our Amazon Book Series page for your copy:

https://www.amazon.com/dp/B0DHP39P5J

The RELATIONSHIP CHARACTERISTICS of a Jesus Follower:
    Are you right with God?
The ONE ANOTHER INSTRUCTIONS to a Jesus Follower:
    Are you right with one another?
The WORSHIP of a Jesus Follower:
    Is your worship acceptable or in vain?
The PRAYER of a Jesus Follower:
    What Scripture says about unleashing the power of God.
The DANGERS of SIN for a Jesus Follower:
    God HATES sin! He abhors sin!
The FOCUS for a Jesus Follower:
    Keep your eyes fixed on Jesus!
The HEART Requirements of a Jesus Follower:
    Follow with all your heart, mind, body, and soul!
The COMMITMENTS of a Jesus Follower:
    Practical Christian living and discipleship.
The OBEDIENCE Requirements for a Jesus Follower:
    Ignore at your own risk!

"Get Wisdom Publishing creates wisdom-driven products that equip readers with timeless insights, understanding, and actionable tools to transform their lives."

Life Planning Series

Read these books if you want to live a better life.

The primary audience for this series is the secular self-help market, but the concepts are Christian based.

CHOOSE FAITH	**For the spiritual seeker and those with spiritual questions.** *Your Spiritual Guidebook For Questions About Religion, God, Heaven, Truth, Evil, and the Afterlife.* https://www.amazon.com/dp/1952359473
CHOOSE CORE VALUES	**Core values will drive your life.** https://www.amazon.com/dp/195235949X

Other Titles in the Life Planning Series
CHOOSE Integrity
CHOOSE Friends Wisely
CHOOSE The Right Words
CHOOSE Good Work Habits
CHOOSE Financial Responsibility
CHOOSE A Positive Self-Image
CHOOSE Leadership
CHOOSE Love and Family
LIFE PLANNING HANDBOOK A Life Plan Is The Key To Personal Growth https://www.amazon.com/gp/product/1952359325

Go to:

https://www.amazon.com/dp/B09TH9SYC4

to get these books.

Personal Daily Prayer Guide
Prayer Resource and Journal

This is a great resource to kick-start your prayer life!

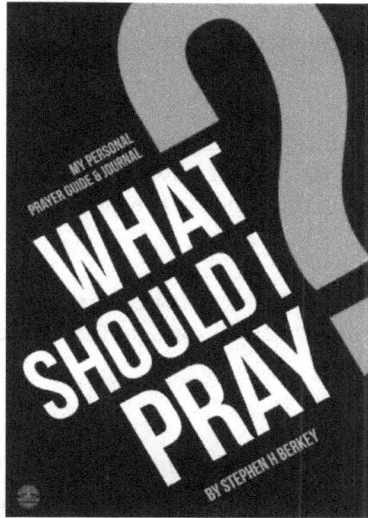

Know what to pray.
Pray based on Bible verses.
Strengthen your prayer life.
Access reference resources.
Pray with eternal implications.
Write your own prayers if desired.
Organize and focus your prayer time.
Learn what the Bible says about prayer.
Find encouragement and advice on how to pray.
Reduce frustration and distraction in your prayer time.

Get your copy today!

Acknowledgments

Arlene
Arlene has served as wife, editor, and proof-reader for all of my writing – thank you for your patience, help, and love.

Michelle
Michelle, our older daughter, has been an invaluable resource. She has graciously produced the website at www.getwisdompublishing.com. She was the first author in the family: graceandthegravelroad.com.

Stephanie
Our middle daughter designed all the covers for the *OBSCURE* Bible Study Series, as well as the marks and logos for Get Wisdom Publishing. We are grateful for her talent!

KOINONIA Small Group
These dear friends have hung in there with me as I taught many of the lessons to them first. Their input, answers, and suggestions have been invaluable.

God, Jesus, and Holy Spirit
Thank you, Lord, for Your guidance and direction.

Notes

SHAMGAR

1. Nelson's Illustrated Bible Dictionary, Copyright © 1986, Thomas Nelson Publishers; from PC Study Bible, "Judges"

2. Nelson's Illustrated Bible Dictionary, Copyright © 1986, Thomas Nelson Publishers; from PC Study Bible, "Judges"

3. International Standard Bible Encyclopedia, revised edition, Copyright © 1979 by Wm. B. Eerdmans Publishing Co.; from PC Study Bible, "Oxgoad;" All rights reserved.

4. Nelson's Illustrated Bible Dictionary, Copyright © 1986, Thomas Nelson Publishers; from PC Study Bible, "Anath"

5. International Standard Bible Encyclopedia, revised edition, Copyright © 1979 by Wm. B. Eerdmans Publishing Co.; from PC Study Bible, "Anath;" All rights reserved.

6. International Standard Bible Encyclopedia, revised edition, Copyright © 1979 by Wm. B. Eerdmans Publishing Co.; from PC Study Bible, "Shamgar;" All rights reserved.

7. International Standard Bible Encyclopedia, revised edition, Copyright © 1979 by Wm. B. Eerdmans Publishing Co.; from PC Study Bible, "Shamgar;" All rights reserved.

Jethro

8. I read about Jethro's leadership principles in Exodus 18:5-27 prior to 2005 and I made some notes without recording the source. Over the past fifteen years I used that concept to develop the twelve principles and discussion questions contained in this study. I have searched the Internet for a number of key phrases and have not been able to identify a source prior to 2005.

Manoah & Wife

9A. Nelson's Illustrated Bible Dictionary, Copyright © 1986, Thomas Nelson Publishers; from PC Study Bible, "Nazirite"

9B. *International* Standard Bible Encyclopedia, revised edition, Copyright © 1979 by Wm. B. Eerdmans Publishing Co.; from PC Study Bible, "Nazirite;" All rights reserved.

10. Nelson's Illustrated Bible Dictionary, Copyright © 1986, Thomas Nelson Publishers; from PC Study Bible, "Angel of the Lord"

11. Smith's Bible Dictionary, PC Study Bible formatted electronic database Copyright © 2003, 2006 by Biblesoft, Inc.; "Angel of the Lord" All rights reserved.

12. Nelson's Illustrated Bible Dictionary, Copyright © 1986, Thomas Nelson Publishers; from PC Study Bible, "Samson"

13. International Standard Bible Encyclopedia, revised edition, Copyright © 1979 by Wm. B. Eerdmans Publishing Co.; from PC Study Bible, "Samson;" All rights reserved.

Hathach

14. Nelson's Illustrated Bible Dictionary, Copyright © 1986, Thomas Nelson Publishers; from PC Study Bible, "sackcloth."

About the Author

Steve attended church as a child and accepted Christ when he was 10 years old. But his walk with Jesus left a lot to be desired for the next 44 years. In 1994 he "wrestled" with God for some period of months and in September of that year totally surrendered his life to Jesus.

In 1996 he was so driven to study God's Word that he attended the Indianapolis campus of Trinity Evangelical Divinity School (Chicago) to earn a Certificate of Biblical Studies. His hunger for God's Word led him to lead and write all his own Bible studies for his small group. He has been an entrepreneur and Bible study leader for the past 30 years.

He is a member of The Church at Station Hill in Spring Hill, TN, a regional campus of Brentwood Baptist (Brentwood TN).

Contact Us

Website:　　www.getwisdompublishing.com
Email:　　info@getwisdompublishing.com

Facebook:　　Get Wisdom Publishing

Author's Page:　　www.amazon.com/author/stephenhberkey

Amazon's Obscure Bible Study Series page:
https://www.amazon.com/dp/B08T7TL1B1

"Go beyond devotionals.
Experience biblical wisdom in action!"